CW00758435

An Introduction To The Valor Ecclesiasticus Of King Henry Viii

~~t, (eett, ~~~~~~ ~~~~~~~

AN

·INTRODUCTION

TO THE

VALOR ECCLESIASTICUS

OF

KING HENRY VIII.

WITH

A MAP OF ENGLAND AND WALES,

SHOWING

THE DISTRIBUTION IN DIOCESES.

By The Rev. JOSEPH HUNTER, F.S.A.

PRINTED BY COMMAND

OF

HIS MAJESTY KING WILLIAM IV.

IN PURSUANCE OF AN ADDRESS OF

THE HOUSE OF COMMONS OF GREAT BRITAIN;

AND UNDER THE DIRECTION OF

THE COMMISSIONERS ON THE PUBLIC RECORDS

OF THE KINGDOM.

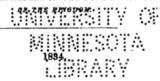
UNIVERSITY OF MINNESOTA LIBRARY

1834.

UNIVERS
MINNF

COMMISSIONERS

ON

THE PUBLIC RECORDS OF THE KINGDOM,

APPOINTED BY

HIS MAJESTY'S COMMISSION

OF THE

12th of March 1831.

HIS GRACE THE ARCHBISHOP OF CANTERBURY.

THE RIGHT HONOURABLE THE LORD CHANCELLOR.

THE RIGHT HONOURABLE THE SECRETARY OF STATE FOR THE HOME DEPARTMENT.

THE RIGHT HONOURABLE THE SPEAKER OF THE HOUSE OF COMMONS.

THE RIGHT HONOURABLE THE CHANCELLOR OF THE EXCHEQUER.

THE RIGHT HONOURABLE THE MASTER OF THE ROLLS.

THE RIGHT HONOURABLE THE LORD CLERK REGISTER OF SCOTLAND.

THE RIGHT HONOURABLE EARL SPENCER, K. G.

THE RIGHT HONOURABLE THE EARL OF ABERDEEN, K. T.

THE RIGHT REVEREND THE LORD BISHOP OF LLANDAFF.

THE RIGHT HONOURABLE THOMAS GRENVILLE.

THE RIGHT HONOURABLE CHARLES WATKIN WILLIAMS WYNN, M. P.

THE RIGHT HONOURABLE SIR JAMES MACKINTOSH.

THE RIGHT HONOURABLE HENRY HOBHOUSE.

THE RIGHT HONOURABLE LORD DOVER.

THE HONOURABLE MR. JUSTICE PARKE.

THE HONOURABLE MR. JUSTICE BOSANQUET.

SIR ROBERT HARRY INGLIS BART., M. P.

LOUIS HAYES PETIT ESQUIRE.

HENRY BELLENDEN KER ESQUIRE.

HENRY HALLAM ESQUIRE.

JOHN ALLEN ESQUIRE.

EDWARD PROTHEROE ESQUIRE.

EDWARD VERNON UTTERSON ESQUIRE.

WILLIAM BROUGHAM ESQUIRE, M. P.

CHARLES PURTON COOPER ESQUIRE, SECRETARY.

A 2

The publication of the Valor is in Six Folio Volumes. The present Introduction was prepared for that work, and is inserted among the Prefatory Matter in the First Volume. It is here republished in a more convenient form, and a few Notes and Illustrations touching the subjects treated of in it have been added.

INTRODUCTION

TO THE

VALOR ECCLESIASTICUS

OF

KING HENRY VIII.

———

THE pre-eminence amongst the Ecclesiastical Records of the Kingdom must on every ground be conceded to the VALOR ECCLESIASTICUS of King Henry VIII. It is no less than an entire Survey and Estimate of the whole Ecclesiastical Property of England and Wales, in the state in which it stood on the very eve of the Reformation,—the accumulation of the many centuries which had preceded since first the British Church was endowed. The importance, politically and historically, of such a document was early perceived and acknowledged by His Majesty's Commissioners on the Public Records of the Realm. At an early period of their labours they directed that it should be transcribed and printed, committing the execution of the work to their late Secretary, Mr. Caley. The work

Important character o the Valor.

A 4

Printing: the order
and progress. has been long in progress. The First Volume
appeared in 1810; the Second in 1814; and
this was followed by three other Volumes,
which were published respectively in 1817,
1821, and 1825.[1]

All of this Record which could then be
found in the Office of the First Fruits, to
which the custody of it is committed, was then
laid before the Public; and nothing more
seemed to be wanting to complete the design
which was laid down in the First Volume,
except a suitable Introduction which should
show the History, Nature, Use, and State of
the Record, and a General Map of England
and Wales, presenting at one view the great
Ecclesiastical Divisions of the country.

Supplementary matter
in Vol. VI. It happened, however, that some detached
pieces of evidence, which, if not actual portions
of the Valor, are contemporary with it, and
contain information of the same description,
were discovered about that time at the Augmentation Office and the Chapter House.[2]
A very distinguished Member of the former
Commissions, now deceased, also suggested
that a General Index would give additional
value and efficiency to the publication. So
that it was resolved that a Sixth Volume
should be prepared, to consist of the newly-
discovered Documents and a General Index,

[1] See NOTE A. p. 37.   [2] See NOTE B. p. 37.

and that with it should appear the Map and the Introduction, which were promised in the First Volume.

The Commissioners named in the Royal Commission of March 12, 1831, found the Sixth Volume in an unfinished state. The whole of the documentary matter was printed, as was also a considerable part of the Index; but no preparation had been made for the Map or for the General Introduction.

It is to be regretted that these, and particularly the latter, had not been executed by the Editor, who had advantages for such a work which the Writer of the present Introduction cannot be expected to possess. It is fortunate, however, that the history of the Valor is not one of those obscure subjects which require for their perfect elucidation to have light thrown upon them drawn from many and distant quarters; nor does the arrangement or any part of the contents of the Record present any insurmountable or considerable difficulties.

All that seems to belong to a suitable Introduction to this Record may be distributed under the following Heads :—

I. The Purpose for which the Valor was formed.

II. The Manner of Proceeding in making it.

III. What Classes of Dignities, Benefices, and Ecclesiastical Foundations were within its scope.

IV. The Mode in which the Property is set forth.

V. The Uses now to be made of the Valor.

VI. Its State, Conservation, and Publication.

And in this order it is now proposed to proceed.

I.—*The Purpose for which the Valor was formed.*

Origin of the Valor.

This purpose is to be sought for in the measures incident to the Reformation of Religion under King Henry VIII.

Usurpations of the Church of Rome.

During a long series of ages the usurpations of the Church of Rome on the ancient freedom and property of the English Church had been advancing, till they had reached a height which may justly be called enormous. Some small contribution might seem to be not unreasonably demanded from every part of Christendom by that Power, which by common consent, or at least common submission, was supposed to be ever consulting for the common benefit of Christianity, and which did actually administer the affairs of the great Christian confederacy. But the contributions demanded were grown excessive ; they were

claimed on every pretence; and there was also
much of delay and vexation in consequence of
the demands.

Resistance to these encroachments had been
made from time to time by the Sovereigns
and the Prelates and Nobles. The claim
to Annates, which, as we shall see, was inti-
mately connected with the matter contained
in the Valor, had been declared by an Act of
Henry IV.'s Parliament to be " a horrible
mischief and damnable custom ;"— and other
portions of the claims had been often made a
subject of negotiation and dispute.

Annates: resistance
to them.

At length, however, the cord was completely
cut which bound the English Church to that
of Rome. Under King Henry VIII. the
demands were questioned in a spirit of the
most unlimited freedom ; the unsoundness of
the title and the political inexpediency were
made apparent; and the Church of Rome was
deprived, not only of Annates, but of the
whole of that revenue which she had been
accustomed to derive from England.

While the negotiations were proceeding respecting the divorce, the Parliament, which
began to sit at Westminster on the 15th January, in the Twenty-third year of Henry VIII.
(A.D.1532), passed an Act, entitled "An Acte
concernynge restraynt of payment of Annates
to the See of Rome." The use of the term An-

nates in this Act is evident from the Act itself. It described the First Fruits of the Bishopricks and Archbishopricks, with all sums paid for Palls, Bulls, and the like, on the consecration of every new Prelate. Nothing is said in the Act of any Tenths paid to the Pope; or of any, either First Fruits or Tenths, from any person holding Dignity or Benefice below the dignity of Bishop. This seems to have been in some measure overlooked by previous writers on this subject, who seem to have considered the Annates, of which by this Act the Pope was deprived, as being that which by a subsequent Act was given to the King. The sums received under the denomination of Annates from the Second year of King Henry VII., a period of forty-five years, are said in the Act to have been not less than £160,000. The further payment of Annates is restrained under the severe penalty of the forfeiture of all his temporalities by any Bishop or Archbishop who should in this offend. A new mode is pointed out for the consecration of Prelates : and it is declared, that in case the Pope should resort to an Interdict, Divine Service should notwithstanding proceed as it had been accustomed.

Annates : what.

Pope deprived of them.

Yet the Act did not quite close the door to an amicable arrangement on the subject of this claim. The King was empowered to negotiate for the moderation of the demand, and to give or withhold his consent to the Act itself till the meeting of the next Parliament. One object plainly was to strengthen the King's hands in his negotiations concerning the divorce, by empowering him, without again going to Parliament, to cut off at his own pleasure this great source of the Papal Revenue.

One object to strengthen the King in his negotiations with Rome.

It was not till the 25th of July 1533 that the King ratified the Act. Whether there was supposed to have been any irregularity in this, or any departure from the principles of the English Constitution, another Act upon the subject was thought necessary; and accordingly, when Parliament again met, which it did on the 15th January 1534, a second Act was passed, in which the main provisions of the former Act are ratified, and in which the King's ratification of it by his Letters Patent is recognized and confirmed. This Act forms the twentieth chapter of the Acts of the Twenty-fifth of Henry VIII.; and the very next Act goes farther in the same course, declaring it to be unlawful to make any payments on any pretence to the See of Rome, and severing the connection which had existed between the two states.

Second Act on the subject.

Separation of England from Rome.

The people and clergy of England were by these Acts relieved from a heavy burthen. But it was not in the contemplation of the Court to give to the Church what it had wrested from the Pope, without requiring something in return. The Court could not demand from the Church the Annates, the Peter Pence, the Indulgence Fees, and other moneys under the old names: some other form it was necessary to adopt. What might be the principle of the commutation it may not now be easy to discover, but the demand at last assumed this form,—that the Church should render to the King the First Fruits of all Benefices and Dignities, and the Tenth of their Annual Revenues.[3]

First Fruits and Tenths given to the King.

This was settled by an Act passed in the Parliament which began to sit on the 3d November, in the Twenty-sixth of Henry VIII. (A.D. 1534.) The title is "An Acte concerninge the paiment of Firste Fruites of all dignities, benefices, and promocyons spirituall, and also concerninge one annuell pencyon of the tenthe parte of all the possessions of the Churche, spirituall and temporall, graunted to the Kinges Highnes and his heires." It forms the third chapter of the Acts of that Parliament, the first having been the Act which declares the King the Supreme Head of the Church of England.

It was to carry into effect the provisions of this Act that the Valor was formed.

First Fruits and Tenths: what.

The First Fruits are declared to be the clear revenue and profits for one entire year;

---

[3] See NOTE C. p. 39.

and the Tenths, the tenth part of such clear
annual revenue. They were to be taken of all
" Archbishopricks, Bishopricks, Abbeys, Monasteries, Priories, Colleges, Hospitals, Archdeaconries, Deaneries, Provostships, Prebends,
Parsonages, Vicarages, Chantries, Free Chapels,
and every other dignity, benefice, office, or
promotion spiritual within the realm or else-
where within any of the King's dominions, of
what name, nature, or quality soever they be,
or to whose foundation, patronage, or gift
soever they belong."

An Act like this, which gave the King a A Survey necessary.
permanent revenue from a new source, having
no mean ratio to the whole aggregate revenue
of the Crown, required some preparation to
carry it into effect; and in particular it became necessary to ascertain what and how
many ecclesiastical foundations there were
which stood affected by the provisions of the
Act, and what was the amount of the annual
revenue from each to which the King was
entitled.

There was indeed already existing of record
in the King's Exchequer a Valor of the Ecclesiastical Property of England. This had
been made in the time of King Edward I.
under the sanction of Pope Nicholas IV. It
had been used as the standard by which all
assessments on the Clergy were regulated, and
all papal or regal demands. Even now it is of

use in the interpretation of the Statutes of some Colleges founded before the Reformation. But for so great a purpose as the determining a fixed perpetual annual payment, beside the casual payment on every avoidance, a new Survey and Valuation seemed expedient, if not absolutely necessary : for (1.) a great change had taken place in the value, as estimated in money, of most of the dignities and benefices, probably of all : (2.) a great change had taken place in their relative values[4]: and (3.) there had arisen in the interval between the date of Pope Nicholas' Valor and the time of this Act innumerable foundations of the species denominated Chantries, from which a large revenue was about to be derived.[5] The piety of the English nation had flowed very much in that direction in the interval between the reigns of Edward and Henry. The taste for founding the more splendid monastic institutions had declined ; but Chantries had arisen in almost every Church, where, in solemn commemorations of the departed, there was a beautiful union of piety to God, with some of the dearest charities of life.

Hence a new Survey was necessary ; a Survey which should extend to all foundations spiritual whatsoever ; a Survey which should supersede the old Survey as matter of record, and be from henceforth the standard to which

[4] See NOTE D. p. 39.　　　[5] See NOTE E. p. 40.

reference was to be made in all points touching the revenue of the Church, and the contributions it should make to the State; and to which the King or the Clergy might at any time have recourse for the determination of any question that might arise touching the just extent of the demand and render of First Fruits and Tenths. And accordingly in the same Act in which this share of the profits of promotions spiritual is given to the King, his heirs and successors, it is enacted that such a *Commission for the purpose.* Survey shall be taken by Commissioners sent in the King's name into every part of the Kingdom of England and Wales, whose duty it should be to inquire out all such promotions, and to return an exact account of all the temporalities and spiritualities with which they were endowed.

The VALOR ECCLESIASTICUS of King Henry VIII. is the Return into the Exchequer which these Commissioners made.

II.—*The Manner of Proceeding in making the Survey.*

" It is ordeyned and enacted by auctoryte *Clauses of the Act appointing the Commission.* aforesaide, that the Chauncelour of Englande for the tyme beynge, shall have power and auctoryte to dyrecte ynto everie Dyoces yn thys Realme and yn Wales severall Commys-

B

sions yn the Kynge's name, under his greate seale, as well to the Archbusschoppe or Busshoppe of everie such Dyoces as to such other parsone or parsones as the Kynge's Highnes shall name and appoynte, comaundynge and auctorisinge the said Commyssioners so to be named in everie suche Commyssion, or III of them at the leaste, to examyn, serche, and enquyre, by all the wayes and meanes that they can by their dyscrecions, of and for the true and just, hole and entyere yerely values of all the manors, londes, tenements, hereditaments, rents, tythes, offerings, emoluments, and all other profittes aswell spirituall as temporall apperteyninge or belonginge to any Archebusshopricke, &c. within the lymyttes of their Commyssion."

"And it is ordeyned and enacted by auctoryte aforesaide, that the saide Commyssioners shall have full power and auctoryte to do, accomplyssche, and execute the effects and contents of theyr said Commyssions in every behalf; and that every the said Commyssioners before they shall execute their sayd Commyssion shall receyve and take a corporall othe before the Lord Chauncelour, or before suche other as shalbe appoynted by the said Chauncellour by the Kynge's writ of Dedimus Potestatem, that they shall diligently and truly, without favour, affeccion, fraude, covyn, mede, drede, or corrupcion, do, fulfill, and execute the hole effectes and contentes expressid yn everie suche Commyssion, within the lymytts therof, to their connynge, witts, and uttermost of their power."

The oath which the Commissioners were required to take may be found at p. 1. of the Second Volume, and the Commission at p. 289 of the same Volume. From neither of these documents can more be collected than from the preceding extracts from the Act of Parliament, except that the date of the Commissions was on the 30th day of January, in the Twenty-sixth of the King, A. D. 1535, and that the Returns were to be made into the Exchequer by the Octaves of the Holy Trinity. In various portions of the Record we find the names of those who were put in the Commissions, all of whom appear to have been principal persons in their respective district, below the degree of a Baron.[6]

With the Commissions were delivered copies of certain " Instructions" signed by the King. These are printed immediately following this Introduction ; and we may collect from them information concerning the manner in which the Commissioners were to proceed.

The King's "Instructions."

First of all they were to send for any Scribes or Officers of the Bishops or Archdeacons who might be supposed capable of giving them in-

[6] See NOTE F. p. 40.

B 2

formation, and learn from them what Deaneries Rural there were within the limits of the district over which their inquiry was to extend, and to what Diocese or other jurisdiction the said several Deaneries belonged; and then what Deaneries, Monasteries, Benefices, or other Promotions spiritual there were within the limits of their Commission. With this information before them, they were next to divide themselves into parties of three, or some number above three, and each party was to take to itself a certain number of the Deaneries Rural, or other exempt places, at their discretion, and proceed to examine into the value of all spiritual promotions contained therein, according to the lists which had been prepared. And for the better execution of their duty they are directed to examine all Incumbents, their Receivers and Auditors, on oath, and to search all Register books of Accompt, Easter-books, and other writings which may be thought necessary by them, and to use all other ways and means to come at the truth. But in the examination into the value of every Bishoprick, the Bishop is himself to form one of the Commissioners. When they have obtained all the information that is to be had, they are to enter it in a book of accompt, made after the Auditors' fashion. The several parties are then to assemble and compare their several books, which are to be certified together into the King's Exchequer, within the

time limited in the Commission, together with
the Commission itself and the Instructions.

Such was the care taken for the due execution of the duty of which this Record is the
result.

III.—*The Classes of Dignities, Benefices, and Ecclesiastical Foundations within the scope of the Survey.*

The terms of the Act are as comprehensive
as possible. From the Archbishop and the
wealthiest Abbot down to the meanest Vicarage
or the most poorly endowed Chantry, all were
brought within the scope of the Act. But it
may be proper to set the various Promotions
Spiritual before the Reader in the order in
which they are to be found in the Instructions
given to the Commissioners:

All Ecclesiastical Preferments within the scope of the Survey.

I. The See of every Archbishop or Bishop.

II. The Church or Monastery which was
the Seat of any such Archbishop or
Bishop ; and therein the endowments
on any Dean or Prior, Treasurer,
Residencer, Chanter, Sexton, Almoner, Hospitaller, Bowser, or any
other person who has any dignity,
prebend, vicarship, petticanonship,
or other office, chantry, cure, or promotion spiritual in succession.

III. Archdeaconries, and Deaneries Rural.

IV. Colleges, and Churches Collegiate, with
the endowments on the Deans, Sub-
Deans, Masters, Provosts, Prebenda-
ries, Fellows, Brethren, and Chantry
Priests, and every person that has
any dignity, prebend, petticanonship,
or other office, chantry, cure, office,
or other promotion spiritual going by
succession.

V. Hospitals, and Places Conventual of any
Secular Priests or Lay Brethren, with
the endowments on the Master, Pro-
vost, or other Chief Governor, and
on every other person who hath any
dignity, fellowship, brothership, sis-
tership, office, chantry, cure, ad-
vantage, or other promotion spiritual
going by succession.

VI. Abbies, Monasteries, Priories, or Houses
Religious and Conventual, including
Charter Houses (which are expressly
named as claiming, it is said, some
right of exemption), with the endowments on the Abbot or Abbess, Prior
or Prioress, or other Chief Governor,
and also on the Sub-Prior, Sub-
Prioress, Sexton, Selerer, Almoner,
Bowser, Hospitaller, Monk-bailiff,
Canon-bailiff, and every other spiritual person connected with them.

VII. Parsonages, Vicarages, Chantries, and
Free Chapels : of which the former

were benefices not impropriate; the second, churches where was a Vicar having an ordained income. Chantries were private foundations for the commemoration of the dead; and by Free Chapels appear to have been understood those chapels which had been founded within parishes by the devotion of parishioners living usually remote from their parish church, and which had no endowment but what was of the gift of the founders or other benefactors.

All these were to be set down in the books in the following order: First, the See of the Bishop or Archbishop; next the Endowments on the various Offices in the Cathedral Church; and then the Archdeaconries, and Deaneries Rural, with their claims; after this each Rural Deanery in order, with, first, the Monasteries or Colleges within it, and then the various Parsonages, Vicarages, Chantries, and Free Chapels.

<small>In what order to be set down in the Books.</small>

IV.—*The Mode in which the Property is set forth.*

We find in the Act of Parliament, that the Commissioners were required to make a Return of all the fixed Property belonging to any Benefice or Dignity, as manors, lands, tenements, rents; of all the Tithe Property;

<small>Kinds of property.</small>

B 4

and of all the Customary Oblations, which were, as we find, estimated communibus annis: of these the gross amount was to be returned. From this amount, however, they were allowed to make certain deductions before the value was ascertained, which was to be taken as the actual value of the Benefice or Dignity on which the First Fruits and Tenths were to be levied. These deductions consisted of (1.) the Rents resolute to the Chief Lords, and all other annual and perpetual rents and charges: (2.) the Alms which were due to the Poor, according to any foundation or ordinance: (3.) Fees to Stewards, Receivers, Bailiffs, and Auditors: and (4.) Synodals and Procurations, with which most Abbies and Benefices were charged. But the Instructions go in this point beyond the Act; and it being foreseen that claims might be set up for remuneration for Spiritual Services, the Commissioners are strictly enjoined to make no allowance for these; and, with a less appearance of equity, to suffer no estimate of Repairs of Edifices to be taken into account when settling the clear annual income to be derived from them.

Deductions to be allowed.

Conformity of the Record.

The Returns are in general made conformably to these Instructions. In the account of the possessions of the Monasteries, for instance, we have first the annual value of the precincts; next of the lands which were situated in the county in which the house stood; the lands in

other counties; and last the impropriate rectories: and on the other hand, the rents resolute, the alms, the fees, and the synodals. So
in the accounts of the Benefices, we have in
the unimpropriate parishes an account of the
value of the manse, glebe, and tythe (the
value of each particular tythe being often set
forth), with the oblations: and in the impropriate, the sources of the Vicar's income; while
the other portions of the profits are accounted
for by the Religious Houses to which the benefice was appropriated. From both these is
the allowed reduction, which in the case of
the Benefices is seldom more than the Synodals to the Archbishop and the Procurations
to the Archdeacon. The Chantries and the
Free Chapels have their less complex endowments plainly set forth.

The execution of a work of this magnitude *When the Survey was made.*
required, we may suppose, in some instances,
more time than the terms of the Commission
allowed. Yet in general it appears to have
been executed between January and June in
1535. The returns however for the County
of Lincoln are dated on the 3d of September
in that year, and for the County of Bucks on
the 26th of September.

There is not, I believe, any reason to sup- *Faithfully executed.*
pose that the Commissioners did not execute
their work faithfully. In one instance we have
a kind of double return. It will be found in

Vol. i. pp. 89-98, and relates to the Diocese of
Canterbury, of which the Archbishop (Cran-
mer) was required to make a return by the
King's writ, dated 20th July, in the Twenty-
eighth of the King. There are also Returns
made of the Endowments on Officers in the
Church of Wells in the time of Edward VI.
and of Elizabeth, to remedy, as it seems, the
imperfections of the Valor. See it in Vol. i.
p. 129. There is also a double Return of the
Abbey of Burton, Vol. iii. p. 147. But I have
not met with any complaints of remissness or
of oppression; and the great complaint in after
times, when the system of which this book is
the basis was in full operation, was that the
oblations were rated somewhat too highly: the
oblations being in some measure voluntary payments, and being greatly reduced in amount
after the Reformation. See what Fuller says
on this subject in his Church History of Britain, Cent. xvi. B. v. p. 228.[7]

Double Returns.

One complaint.

V. — *The Uses now to be made of this Record.*

Uses —
I. Politically:
1. To determine the First Fruits and Tenths.

And here undoubtedly the first and principal use to be made of it is still that for
which purpose the Survey was undertaken,—
the determining the sums payable as the First
Fruits and Tenths of the Benefices and Dignities which are still chargeable with the payment of them.

[7] See NOTE G. p. 41.

These payments are, however, no longer made to the Crown. Queen Anne, as an act of Royal Bounty to the Church, in the second year of her reign, gave up this source of revenue ; not, indeed, giving it back to the hands which had to render it, but to Trustees, who were empowered to administer it for the benefit of the poorer Clergy. This gift of the Queen was confirmed by Act of Parliament 2 & 3 Anne, cap. 11.

These given back to the Church by Queen Anne.

It is now therefore no longer to be considered as a Record between the King and the Church, but between one portion of the Church and another, as regulating the claims of the Trustees of the Royal Bounty of Queen Anne on the parties who remain chargeable with the render.

But long before the time of this gift the Record had lost something of its importance in this view of it, in consequence of various Acts of Parliament :

Diminution of its importance under this head, by various Acts of Parliament.

And 1. Those by which the Monasteries were dissolved. When the whole revenues were seized by the Crown, there was no longer any room for the claim of fractional portions of them.

2. The Act of the first of Edward VI., which suppressed all the Chantries and some of the Free Chapels, and gave the whole of the revenue by which they were supported to the King.

3. Queen Elizabeth, in the first year of her reign, by the Act by which she repealed a statute of the reign of her predecessor introducing some modifications into the law of First Fruits and Tenths, discharged for ever from the payment of First Fruits all Parsonages which were under the value of 10 marks, and all Vicarages under the value of £10 ; and of both, the Universities, the Colleges of Eton and Winchester, all Hospitals founded for the relief of the poor, and all Schools for the instruction of the young.

And 4. Soon after the gift which Queen Anne had made, there was an Act of Parliament in the sixth of her reign, discharging from the payment of both First Fruits and Tenths all Livings which were then under the annual value of £50.

So that the utility of the Record in respect of that which was the primary object for which it was formed is greatly diminished : those portions of it being in this point of view only of use which relate to the wealthier Rectories and Vicarages, and to such Dignities and high Promotions spiritual, as survived in the new modelling of the Church at the time of the Reformation.

2. Standard value of Dignities and Benefices.

Next to this in point of dignity and importance is, that this Record is taken as exhibiting the value of any piece of Church-preferment, in the interpretation of rights or restrictions

under any subsequent statute in which the
value is a criterion. In this relation it is that
we find the Record often cited under the
name of THE KING'S BOOKS.

And next to this, that it shows what
Churches were of antient foundation, enjoying
tythe as of common right, thereby operating
to maintain in its purity the parochial distribution of the country, and to maintain the
rights of the parish churches against the
chapels, sometimes, but as it seems impro-
perly, called parochial. While amongst chapels
it shows which existed before the Reformation, for it is held that none escaped which
had before the Reformation any fixed endowment : whence it follows that any Chapel not
in this book is either of recent foundation, or
was left by its founders without any endowment on the priest who was to officiate in it.

3. Showing what
Churches are parochial.

But for practical purposes it is supposed that
there is more frequent resort to this Record
for another purpose. In questions respecting
the profits of Benefices, it is often the best
resort which the parties have ; and in all cases
where the Ordination of a Vicarage is not to
be found in the Depository which ought to
have it in custody, the want of it is best supplied by the matter of this Record : and being
matter of Record it may be pleaded in evidence
in all questions such as these.

4. Showing Endow-
ments.

5. In cases of extinct foundations.

Even those portions of the Valor which by the suppression of the Monasteries and Chantries have in a great measure lost their political importance, are often found valuable in questions of right, showing as they do the estates of the Monasteries, or the rights of tythe enjoyed by the Monasteries; the former of which were often entitled to certain exemptions, and the other it being not less important to ascertain with precision, though they may be now secularized.

So that in its bearing on claims litigated or subject to be litigated, this Record may justly be called inestimable.

II. Historically:

But while the suppression of the Monasteries, Hospitals, Colleges, and Chantries, the foundations of our remote and pious ancestors, and the discharge of so many benefices from the burthen imposed on them, do in some measure lower the importance of the Valor as a document to be used in the public affairs of the country, and the private relations between man and man, yet do not these things at all diminish its value when it is looked at under that other aspect under which all Records admit of being placed,— as an Historical Document, by means of which much may be collected concerning the state of the country at the time when it was prepared, and many facts be recovered in the transactions of pre-

ceding centuries. Its value in this point of
view will be at once apparent when it is re-
collected that we have here presented before
us, in one grand conspectus, the whole Ecclesiastical Establishment of England and Wales,
as it had been built up in successive centuries,
and when it was carried to its greatest height.
As in Domesday Book we are presented with
a view of the feudal distributions of England
as they were settled at the Conquest, so here
we have the ecclesiastical distributions as they
existed, not only at the time when this survey
was made, but as they had existed, scarcely
altered, from the close of the reign of King
Henry I.:[8] and as in Domesday Book we are
presented with the value of the tenures, and
of particular species of property attached to
them, so here we have the valuation of the
various dignities and benefices, and of the
particular species of property with which they
were endowed. So that we at once see, not
only the antient extent and amount of that
provision which was made by the piety of the
English nation for the spiritual edification of
the people by the erection of Churches and
Chapels for the decent performance of the
simple and touching ordinances of the Christian Religion, but how large a proportion had
been saved from private appropriation of the
produce of the soil, and how much had sub-
sequently been given, to form a public fund,

1. Shows the whole
Ecclesiastical Esta-
blishment as it stood
on the eve of the
Reformation.

[8] See NOTE H. p. 41.

accessible to all, out of which might be supported an order of cultivated and more enlightened men dispersed through society, and by means of which blessings incalculable might be spread amongst the whole community. If there were spots or extravagancies, yet on the whole it is a pleasing as well as a splendid spectacle, especially if we look with minute observation into any portion of the Record, and compare it with a map which shows the distribution of population in those times over the island, and then observe how Religion had pursued man even to his remotest abodes, and was present among the most rugged dwellers in the hills and wildernesses of the land, softening and humanizing their hearts.

All this is interesting to the Philosopher as well as to the Historian; while it is of essential importance to him who undertakes to give a topographical description of any portion of the country: but the Record does not stop here. It presents us with a view of those more gorgeous establishments where the service of the Most High was conducted in the magnificent structures which still exist amongst us, with a great array of priests, and all the pomp of which acts of devotion admit; and of the Abbies and other Monasteries, now but ruined edifices, where resided the sons and daughters of an austerer piety, and where the services were scarcely ever suspended.

But when it sets forth the sources from 2. Innumerable facts and persons occur in it. whence the revenue was derived by which these foundations were maintained, and the outgoings from the rents and profits, charges for obits and alms, settled often by the original founder, we are presented with innumerable facts, important in monastic history, and in the history of the persons who were distinguished in the reigns of our early Sovereigns. While in the full enumeration which is given of the various persons who held offices in the Monasteries, as Auditors, Stewards, and Receivers, we have facts which the Biographer may turn to excellent account in the lives of many persons who flourished in the reigns of the Tudors ; and in the accounts of Benefices and Dignities an almost complete catalogue of the Clergy of that time, with the several preferments enjoyed by them, — a time of such peculiar importance in the Ecclesiastical History of the country.

And, lastly, the notices of the Chantries in 3. Chantry Chapels. this Record serve as the best guide we have to the purpose and the æra of those Chapels which we find attached to so many of the parish Churches of England, injuring their symmetry, and obscuring the original design, but often presenting features of great architectural beauty, and of which, by aid of this Record, the age may not unfrequently be determined.

VI.—*The State, Conservation, and Publication of the Record.*

It will be seen, by reference to the King's Instructions, that the Commissioners were to make their Returns according to the fashion of Auditors' Books. In the manner in which the accompts are drawn up, they have done so, but in the form in which they have rendered the accompts there is great diversity. Some of the Commissioners made their returns on rolls, some in books; some on paper, others on parchment.

Irregular form in which the Returns were made.

Injuries.

A Record thus irregular in its form and various in its material is more exposed to injury and loss than when it consists of a series of rolls or volumes of the same form and material. And paper, especially when in rolls, is a far less suitable material for the purpose than parchment, which is often seen rendering up its trust with perfect fidelity after the lapse of ten or twelve centuries, and promising to render it with equal fidelity to the men of centuries yet distant. The paper rolls of this Record have sustained some injury; but they are now protected from further injury by having been bound in volumes under the especial superintendence of Mr. Caley. What rolls still remain in their original form are preserved in the best manner possible, by being placed in cases of tin.

And now, an unfortunate confession is to be made :—Some portions of the Record are lost. Among these is the whole Diocese of Ely; a great part of the Diocese of London; the Counties of Berks, Rutland, and Northumberland; much of the Returns for the Diocese of York, including the whole Deaneries of Rydal and Craven. That Returns for these districts did once exist is made manifest by the book preserved in the same office, entitled LIBER VALORUM. In this book are transcribed the names of the dignities and benefices, with the value of each, but without the particulars. It was made long ago, for the use of the office, when the Record was entire. Where the Record itself is wanting, this Book has been used in the present publication.

It is however but an imperfect remedy to a loss which is greatly to be deplored, as it deprives the country of some of the most valuable information that has ever been made matter of Record, and renders so far nugatory the expence and labour of this great Commission. What account may now be given of the time or the circumstances of the disappearance of these documents from the care of those who were the sworn guardians of them, I have no information before me on which to depend;— they are not known to have existed within the memory of any person now connected with the Office :— but I cannot forbear to add that it must give satisfaction to all persons

Much of the Record lost.

How the loss has been supplied.

Loss greatly to be regretted.

who are sensible to the importance of handing down to posterity the matter contained in the more prominent of the National Records, that over what remains, — and it is by far the larger portion of this great work, — a protection is now extended, more secure, more lasting, than the vigilance of the most trustworthy keepers, and the protection of the safest depositories.

Value of the Press, as placing the matter of important Records beyond the reach of accident.

While the Press multiplies and diffuses, it also preserves : and should the other portions of this Record follow those which are gone, it is to be feared, irrecoverably, this printed Work will still remain, and will show the sound policy on which the Government has acted in giving the matter of such an import- ant document to the Press.

Appendix : Integrity of the Record some- what violated in this publication.

An Appendix is annexed to each Volume, consisting of Returns made in 1810, by the Prelates, of places in their respective Dioceses where there exists any Peculiar Jurisdiction : and it must be added that the integrity of the original Record has been so far violated in this publication as to introduce the new diocesal division of the country which was made in the Thirty-fourth of Henry VIII., eight years after the date of this Survey.

JOSEPH HUNTER,
Sub-Commissioner.

30, Torrington Square,
January 25, 1834.

NOTES and ILLUSTRATIONS.

Note A.

The Volumes contain the Dioceses in the following order:

Vol. I. Canterbury: Rochester: Bath and Wells: Bristol: Chichester: London.

II. Winchester: Salisbury: Oxford: Exeter: Gloucester.

III. Hereford: Coventry and Lichfield: Worcester: Norwich: Ely.

IV. Lincoln: Peterborough: Llandaff: St. David's: Bangor: St. Asaph.

V. York: Chester: Carlisle: Durham.

Note B.

These consist of the following articles:

1. A Return which was made to the Commissioners by John Ruste, Dean of the Deanery of Hecham or Hycham in the Diocese of Norwich. This is evidently the information on which the Commissioners proceeded in making the Return of that Deanery, which we find at pp. 372, 373, of the Third Volume, and contains the particulars which composed many of the sums there stated. It can scarcely be regarded as itself any portion of the Valor, and there is no evidence that it was certified as part of the Commissioners' Return for the

Diocese of Norwich; neither indeed how it found its way into the Augmentation Office.

2. A very valuable Return of the particulars of the endowments on the Prior, Sub-Prior, and twelve other officers in the Priory of St. Swithin, Winchester, in which Church was the Seat of the Bishop of the Diocese. The value of this document arises from the Return in the Valor, Vol. II. p. 2, being without any particulars, only certain gross sums being inserted. There is, however, some slight variation between the sums in this document and those in the Valor. And it may be observed that in the General Index, pp. 337, 338, there is a slight oversight, the Cathedral Church of St. Swithin. of Winchester, and the Priory of St. Swithin of Winchester, being entered as distinct and separate foundations, whereas in truth they are one and the same.

3. A fragment (the earlier portions being lost) of the Return for the Monastery of Coggeshall in the Diocese of London. Of the property of this Monastery there was before no account given, except the single line from the Liber Valorum, Vol. I. p. 444, nearly the whole of the Returns of the Diocese of London having been lost.

4. A like Return of the Possessions of the Monastery of Walden in the same Diocese. This and the preceding appear as if they might have been actual portions of the Valor, certified under the hands of the Commissioners.

5. A Particular of the Possessions of the Abbey of Durford in the Diocese of Chichester, made after the dissolution of the House, reciting the Return made by the Commissioners, as at Vol. I. p. 321, and adding to it an account of the Site and Demesne lands, which, contrary to the usual practice, are omitted in the Valor.

6. What appears to be a General Heading, p. xiv., is in fact only the particular heading of the first portion of this

document, which consists of a Table of First Fruits due to the Bishop of Bangor from the churches in his diocese. As to the rest, it appears to consist of miscellaneous information concerning the ecclesiastical foundations in this diocese, collected by the Commissioners, out of which to frame the Return which we have in the Valor.

7. Similar, but less ample, Collections for the Diocese of St. Asaph. There is nothing to show by what means this and the preceding came to be returned into any public office.

NOTE C.

Fuller (Church History, Cent. xvi. B. v. sect. 4.) says that these were formerly paid to the Pope. But see the matter more accurately stated by Blackstone, B. i. ch. viii. sect. 4, though not with so much precision as might be desired. The Pope is said to have claimed the tythe of the tythe, on the principle that the Pastor Pastorum was entitled to Decimas Decimarum. The High Priest of the Jews had the tenth of the tythe which the Levites took. The claim of First Fruits was also founded on the Jewish institutions. Probably there was no attempt at establishing a principle, beyond what these analogies might be supposed to present; nor any very accurate adjustment of what was taken by the Crown to what was wrested from the Pope in favour of the Church, though it seems there was not much reason to complain; and what was now taken was as nothing when compared with the acts of rapacity which soon followed.

NOTE D.

A comparison of a few of the Parsonages in the Deanery of Doncaster and Diocese of York, in the constitution of which

no change is known to have taken place in the interval between
the two Valors, will evince both these facts.

		A.D. 1291.				A.D. 1535.		
		£	s.	d.		£	s.	d.
Bramwith -	-	13	6	8	- -	12	18	4
Sprotborough	-	26	13	4	- -	44	18	8½
Sandal -	-	8	0	0	- -	9	0	1
Armthorpe	-	5	0	0	- -	8	18	8
Burgh-Wallis	-	12	0	0	- -	14	6	10
Smeaton -	-	10	0	0	- -	10	1	0
Badsworth -	-	20	0	0	- -	32	5	8
Thurnscoe	-	5	6	8	- -	11	7	8
Warmesworth	-	5	6	8	- -	6	10	10
Edlington -	-	10	0	0	- -	5	19	0

NOTE E.

There were fifty-two Chantries in the Parish Churches in
the single Deanery of Doncaster, beside many others founded
in the various Chapels in that Deanery. The Cathedral
Churches were crowded with them. Some had splendid
endowments; but of the Rural Chantries, perhaps £5 may be
about the average annual value. The Foundation Charters of
the Chantries commonly contain valuable genealogical information, besides admitting us to a view of the mode in which
the religious spirit of the English nation was wont to manifest
itself most strikingly in the two centuries which preceded the
time of Reformation.

NOTE F.

It has been observed that the names of these Commissioners
serve to show what families were remaining of the antient
Gentry of England at the time of the rise of the new race of
Gentry who were enriched by the Abbey-lands.

NOTE G.

The passage is this :—" No such favour [he had been speaking of the proceedings in a similar Commission in Ireland] was allowed to any place in England, where all were impartially rated, and Vicarages valued very high according to the present revenue by personal perquisites. In that age he generally was the richest Shepherd who had the greatest flock, where Oblations from the living, and Obits for the dead, (as certainly paid as Predial Tythes,) much advanced their income. In consideration whereof, Vicaridges (mostly lying in market-towns and populous parishes) were set very high, though soon after those Obventions sunk with superstition; and the Vicars in vain desired a proportionable abatement in the King's Books, which, once drawn up, were no more to be altered."

NOTE H.

Only few, and those immaterial, changes were made in the Ecclesiastical distribution of England from the close of the reign of Henry I. to the time when, a few years after the date of this Survey, King Henry VIII. founded five new Bishopricks.

The Conqueror found the two Archbishopricks, and the following Bishopricks :

Durham.	Salisbury.	Hereford.
London.	Exeter.	Coventry.
Winchester.	Wells.	Lincoln.
Rochester.	Worcester.	Thetford.
Chichester.		

The seat of the Bishop of Thetford was removed to Norwich in 1088.

King Henry I. founded the See of Ely in 1109; and the See of Carlisle in 1133.

D

King Henry VIII. in 1541, founded the Sees of Bristol,
Gloucester, Oxford, Peterborough, and Chester.

In the Map is shown what portions of the older Dioceses
were taken to form the See of each of the new Bishops.

Nothing is known of the time when the Sees were distributed into Archdeaconries, and the next subdivision, the
Rural Deaneries. This was probably done upon plan and
with design; but the parochial distribution seems to have
obtained the form in which we now see it, and as it existed in
the time of the Valor, in the time of Pope Nicholas IV., and, *1291*
as there is every reason to believe, at the close of the reign of
King Henry I.,—by accident; that is, as the Lords of Manors
were rich enough and devout enough to erect a Church for
the convenient enjoyment of the Christian Ordinances by
themselves, their families, and the population on their Manor
generally. Since the time of Selden it has been the received
opinion that in this gradual manner parishes became formed,
the Bishops, for the encouragement of such acts of piety,
allowing the Lords to subtract their tythe from the Mother
Church, and to settle it upon the Priest in their own newly
founded Church: nor has any more plausible account ever
been proposed. The difficulty is to find a decree which put a
stop to this; and yet there appears not to have been any
founding of parishes after the reign of Henry I., except in
some peculiar circumstances.

Religious edifices, which in earlier times would have been
regarded as parish churches, were erected after the close of
the reign of Henry I., and many of them enjoyed the privi-
lege of a Font and a Burial-ground. To the priest, in some
of them, it was also allowed to pronounce the nuptial bene-
diction. Many such edifices were raised between the reigns
of Henry I. and Henry VIII.; but they never were allowed to
disturb the parochial distribution or to take any portion of
the tythe. That distribution was held to be complete; and it
is indeed a just subject of wonder that in the first century

after the Conquest so many thousands of parish churches should have been erected, as if by simultaneous effort, in every part of the land, while at the same time spacious and magnificent edifices were arising in every diocese to be the seats of the Bishops and Archbishops, or the scenes of the perpetual services of the inhabitants of the Cloister. Saxon piety had done much, perhaps more than we can collect from the pages of Domesday; but it is rather to the Normans than to the Saxons that we are to attribute the great multitude of parish churches existing at so remote an æra; and a truly wise and benevolent exertion of Christian piety the erection of them must be regarded.

LONDON. Printed by George Eyre and Andrew Spottiswoode, Printers to the King's most Excellent Majesty. 1834.

Lightning Source UK Ltd.
Milton Keynes UK
UKHW020627290622
405123UK00005B/418